LeBr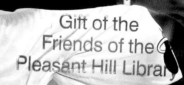n James

Dan Osier

PowerKiDS press
New York

Published in 2011 by The Rosen Publishing Group, Inc.
29 East 21st Street, New York, NY 10010

Copyright © 2011 by The Rosen Publishing Group, Inc.

First Edition

Editor: Amelie von Zumbusch
Book Design: Kate Laczynski

Photo Credits: Cover, p. 1 Jamie Squire/Getty Images Sport/Getty Images; pp. 4, 6–7, 10–11, 18–19 Gregory Shamus/Getty Images; pp. 8–9, 16–17 David Liam Kyle/NBAE/Getty Images; p. 12–13 © Bob Leverone/TSN/Icon SMI; p. 15 Andy Lyons/Getty Images; p. 20 Noah Graham/NBAE/Getty Images; p. 22 D. Clarke Evans/ NBAE/Getty Images.

Library of Congress Cataloging-in-Publication Data

Osier, Dan.
 LeBron James / by Dan Osier. — 1st ed.
   p. cm. — (Basketball's MVPs)
 Includes index.
 ISBN 978-1-4488-2522-6 (library binding) —
 ISBN 978-1-4488-2629-2 (pbk.) — ISBN 978-1-4488-2782-4 (6-pack)
 1. James, LeBron—Juvenile literature. 2. Basketball players—United States—Biography—Juvenile literature. I. Title.
 GV884.J36O75 2011b
 796.323092—dc22
 [B]
                              2010026605

Manufactured in the United States of America

CPSIA Compliance Information: Batch #WW11PK: For Further Information contact Rosen Publishing, New York, New York at 1-800-237-9932

CONTENTS

This is LeBron James. His nickname is King James.

James plays small forward. He **scores** many points for his team.

8

LeBron James is a team leader. He helps his **teammates** play better.

James was born in Akron, Ohio, on December 30, 1984.

11

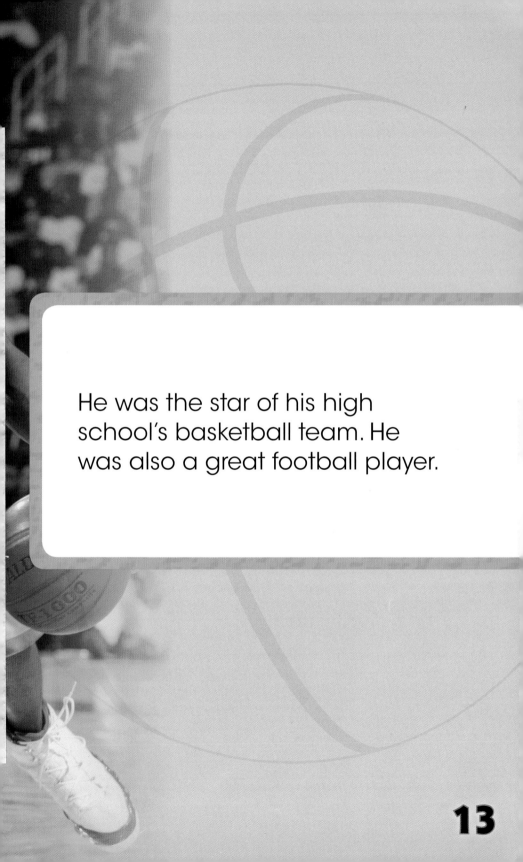

He was the star of his high school's basketball team. He was also a great football player.

In 2003, James finished high school and joined the Cleveland Cavaliers.

15

stillata
CAVALIER
23
DAVIS
34
OfficeMax
OfficeMax
OfficeMax
MAX
MORE

James was young, but he played well. He was named **Rookie** of the Year in 2004.

In 2009, James was named the NBA's most **valuable** player, or MVP.

19

James was named the NBA's MVP yet again in 2010!

That July, he joined the Miami Heat. The team was very happy to have him.

BOOKS

Here are more books to read about LeBron James and basketball:

Feinstein, Stephen. *LeBron James.* African-American Heroes. Berkeley Heights, NJ: Enslow Publishers, Inc., 2008.

Hoffman, Mary Ann. *LeBron James: Basketball Star.* Sports Superstars. New York: PowerKids Press, 2007.

WEB SITES

Due to the changing nature of Internet links, PowerKids Press has developed an online list of Web sites related to the subject of this book. This site is updated regularly. Please use this link to access the list:
www.powerkidslinks.com/bmvp/lebronj/

GLOSSARY

rookie (RU-kee) A new major-league player.

scores (SKAWRZ) Makes points in a game.

teammates (TEEM-mayts) People who play for the same team.

valuable (VAL-yoo-bul) Important.

INDEX